Impossible Thirst

Impossible Thirst

poems
Kathryn de Lancellotti

- 2020 -

Impossible Thirst
© Copyright 2020 Kathryn de Lancellotti
All rights reserved. No part of this book may be used or reproduced in any manner whatsoever without written permission from either the author or the publisher, except in the case of credited epigraphs or brief quotations embedded in articles or reviews.

Editor-in-chief
Eric Morago

Associate Editors
Robin Fiorito & Victoria Lynne McCoy

Editor Emeritus
Michael Miller

Marketing Director
Dania Alkhouli

Marketing Assistant
Ellen Webre

Proofreader
José Enrique Medina

Front cover art
Dakota Pitts

Author photo
Kori Kristine Savoie

Book design
Michael Wada

Moon Tide logo design
Abraham Gomez

Impossible Thirst
is published by Moon Tide Press

Moon Tide Press
6709 Washington Ave. #9297, Whittier, CA 90608
www.moontidepress.com

FIRST EDITION

Printed in the United States of America

ISBN # 978-1-7350278-0-6

Contents

A Daughter's Grief	8
The Boot	9
Not to the Father Will I Give Myself	10
What God Is	12
Notre Dame Was on Fire, but Found Structurally Sound	13
Things We Do	14
Farewell to Jezebel: Eaten by Dogs	16
Figure Study	17
Clay and Pyre	20
Homage to My Period	21
The Astronaut and the Suit	22
These Walls	23
Remember Me	24
The Rain Fell, the Floods Came	26
The First Time	28
Whale Song	29
That Star, Right There	30
That You'd Disappear	31
How It Scattered Across the Lawn Like a Hand Tossing Seed	32
The Meadowlark	34
Water Song	35
Veil of the Flower	36
Cypress Cemetery	37
About the Author	*40*
Acknowledgements	*41*

I dream of a world redefined by its destruction
A beautiful burning

A Daughter's Grief

Sylvia,

Aren't we all looking for a way out of the owl's talons?
A way not to remember
the honeybee's sting, the shape of a boot on your back,
all the nights your breasts would leak, a child,
the sucking, the screaming.
Aren't we all looking for a way not to remember
the poems that cry us to sleep, the little ghosts
we carry in our hands, dare we tell?
Forget the Ativan, the razor, your car in Little River.
You wrote in blood, and for your sacrifice, I thank you,
dear Poetess, dear Mother, you took care of your children
the best you could. I've heard the stories.

You'd swear no gas seeped through the door.
You'd swear you sealed worlds between us.

The Boot
after Sharon Olds' "Sex Without Love"

Every woman adores a fascist, / the boot in the face / the brute / brute heart of a brute like you
— Sylvia Plath

I fucked Professor on my period. Pulled his ears
while he plucked the string out with his teeth.
Told me he wasn't afraid to taste a little blood.

I fucked Father on the church pew.
Hymns torn, almost to nothing—how sweet
the sound. How sweet the blood of the lamb.

How do they do it? Sharon asks,
the ones who make love without love?

I tell her I've done it. Done it on dorm room
carpet. Done Daddy next to Jesus, so many daddies
and false Messiahs. I'm not saying it was beautiful

as ice skaters whirling ice, or bones bowed
inside each other. Think crown of thorns.
Think rust and screw. Think I'm ugly

for punishment, that sometimes a daughter
sticks her head in the oven. Sometimes she comes
to the rock for the slaughter, comes face red as wine, red

as meat, red as a child begging *Daddy,*
Daddy don't leave.

Not to the Father Will I Give Myself

Not to confessionals, nor banks, nor country.
I will not drop bombs, Sir, will not build walls.

No longer will I give myself to bearded musicians,
nor salty surfers. Touch myself instead.

I will not treat Earth the way you treat the feminine.
Will not pour oil into oceans, starve the sacred

polar bear, nor steal ivory from an elephant's face.
It's true, Officer, I told my toddler not to trust you,

that you're a dog off leash. Leaders of War,
of Money, of pussy grabbing, you may not kiss me,

nor choose for me.
I don't pray to Archangel Michael, anymore.

I pray to the Mother, to Mary, and to the other Mary.
Dare I say her name?

Washed his feet with her hair—
Saint Magdalene, teach us to love our clitorises.

Teach us multiple orgasms,
no more faking, ladies. Teach us to say, no,

I don't want to have sex with you,
don't want to make your bed. Go ahead, call me a whore.

You've been hurt, too, little brother,
told to take off your sunflower dress.

What God Is

I don't want to hear what God is
from a book or a capitalist.
A bearded man on a spiritual quest
or from a pulpit.
I don't want to hear about sin
or that desire leads to suffering.
I want a God who is Tantric,
moves slow from toe to crown.
One who appears in fire, in lotus
and between breath.
I want a God who watches
from as far as Sirius, close as skin—
bright star, obsidian.
I want a God who is an artist,
a woman, a man. One who labors
and bleeds, suckles on the afterbirth.
I want a God small enough
to watch the sun fall
into the Pacific.
To climb a eucalyptus,
to ravage a wild blackberry.
A God who takes pride in skinning
the mule deer, finds pleasure
in its helpless sway.
I want God to walk down
the golden staircase
for a taste
of this delicious hell.

Notre Dame Was on Fire, but Found Structurally Sound

The way it went up in flames is a mystery.
The smoke alarm went off, just once, then silence.

Coins clinked in confessional cups, then silence.
Men drank the wine, ate the bread, no, the bodies

of circumcised boys. Silence.
How sweet the sound

of a crackling castle. How fitting,
only the rich talk to God.

This building is falling down, down,
it's falling and I wonder how Fathers stay silent.

The fire ate the evidence (how convenient): little white gowns
lit like wicks from Hell.

Devout Ones, pay your penance.
Fog the mirrors with your prayers, your cries for forgiveness.

I'm done watching the patriarchy burn,
but never fall to the ground.

Done putting their fires out—
the same old news: *The structure remains.*

Things We Do

A mother crushes each bone
in her daughter's foot with a rock
before wrapping it in silk.
She sticks a metal rod in her mouth to save the tongue.
Flat-footed girls never marry.

/

A woman finds a coat hanger deep
inside her closet.
She fishes out every seed until she bleeds.
Here, it's always winter,
fresh powder covers the stains.

/

A girl's thirteenth birthday
today. Her father, the butcher, will sharpen
his blade on a marble slab.
He'll mutilate the clitoris—
prepare for the feast.

/

A daughter dances for her father until the head
of a prophet is served on a silver platter.
She does this for all
who've been silenced in church,
the bedroom, the market. Does this
for the misuse of God's name.

/

A man sees a child standing by a well, desires
to fill his cup, asks for a drink. She pours,
he drinks, wants more,
holds her down
beneath an olive tree, takes her virginity.

/

A god whispers in a man's ear—
demands his first born replaces a lamb.
Do you know what he does to his children?
Think you can run someplace he can't?

/

A friend needed the money, so
she got naked, tied her lover to a chair, cut his hair.
What choice does a woman have?

Farewell to Jezebel: Eaten by Dogs
after a 19th-century painting by John Liston Byam Shaw, "Jezebel, Queen of Israel"

Whoever wrote the Bible wanted you remembered
as the Whore of Israel.
They must have hated you, or something you knew,
or possessed, to give you that title.
You aren't a fighter like Deborah or devoted
like Miriam or nameless like Potiphar's wife.
You didn't steal strength with a haircut,
or bathe naked on a rooftop, or laugh at God.
Each time you spread your legs
you knew exactly what you were doing.
You've known since the first finger,
the first fist, all the fissures
and tarring and tears. The king's dead,
they killed your son, too.
You're not going to hide, are you?
You're going to stare out that window
and take it. You don't even care
what they do with your name,
or with the body, you've already left.
You wanted to be remembered with a pink rose
in your red hair, eyes lined with kohl.

Figure Study

1

I was so used to men staring
I thought it was the price I paid.

2

I used to wear fear like a robe I couldn't drop
before walking on stage, afraid
the artist might capture something I can't see
in my own body or face.
I once stood naked in the middle of a classroom,
blood dripping between my legs.
I did not move, did not wipe it away.
I let it fall to my feet until the timer rang.

3

I learned to stand naked for hours in stillness,
to be the canvas, blank.
To give to the artist what's needed—
mostly shadows and shapes.
A man once told me
I was too beautiful to paint, that there was something
about me he couldn't capture.
I learned at a young age not to give it all away,
that it's better to be muse than mate.
I told him, I felt the same. I can't grasp myself, either,
too good at silence, at restraint.
I'm an artist, I say, the world is too loud,
the body is never still, always churning, bleeding to create.
I want to tell you what it's like
to be cut into marble, hung in a gallery,
frozen in a frame. I want to tell you
what it's like to watch a man mold you in still life,
to let him believe he's your maker as he carves
your ivory waist.
Such desire for the body he has formed.
Such art his hands crave—I want to tell you
what it's like to hold a man in stillness, for hours,
then walk out unscathed.

Clay and Pyre
after David Settino Scott's "Seated Model V" oil on panel

Sometimes, she is clay formed into his image,
or flesh toned oil on canvas, a photograph,
a brushstroke. Sometimes, she is model V,
subject, or childless, perhaps
a child herself, hunched over on the couch,
hips holding the weight of frailty.
Here, in this frame, she does not own her body,
she is the kindling burnt off in the pyre.
When she drops her robe
in the middle of the classroom,
or on the floor of the studio, or to the corner
of a bed, she gives herself to the mystery, to the art,
and he takes her, and makes her his own,
each vertebra, each bone and shade, a mirror
he has chased—a frightened spine
like an arrow through the heart.

Homage to My Period

Each month, lovers bleed from me.
It hurts, every time,
reminds me that love is this:
more flush and death.
Witness unfertilized eggs,
droplets of red in a bowl of milk.
Witness the tissue of your unborn spill out.
A cycle, always back to this:
in prayer nine times a day.
This ache in the belly each time
my son asks about his dad.
Each clot I pass
fills the cup full, the cup empty.
It's how the story always goes
—love, bleed, weep.

The Astronaut and the Suit

My body, you are an animal,
a bloody animal.

Before I left my mother
we made an agreement.

You promised to hold me.
I promised to feed you.

My body, you are the door
my son entered and left.

You grew him
with the discipline of a Rishi

and the efficiency of a watch.
I'm starving but I can't eat

my body, I burn toast
to swallow black.

Chew and chew and chew.

These Walls

One day these walls will become
too full and fall to the floor
like the tick that drank its belly red
and dropped from the dog's ear.
There are invisible webs in every corner
I would have never seen
if not for the black hairs caught
like flies to poison.
I placed my ear to the wall, bees hummed
beneath layers of wallpaper, decades
smoothed over with floral and textures.
When the exterminator smoked the hive,
it fled through the chimney—
an angry cloud over Wagon Wheel Blvd.
The milk, the honey, chamomile, Xanax, weed.
I tried everything. My doctor said,
If you can't sleep, clean.
I did not take his advice.
Instead, I lie in bed awake and listen
to my son's breathing.
To owl song and cat fight.
I drift with the night blooming jasmine
into half-dream—
frantically eating my way out
of silk and night, with no choice
but wings
and piercing light.

Remember Me

the blue baby
on the sands of Italy
the mother on the floor
who weeps?
I'm the one who changed—
plucked the fruit
made love to a snake.
Sold my body
absorbed poison in the factory
hid in the desert for days.
I look in the mirror
see nothing.
Can't make a living
or leave.
I'm Sarah laughing at God.
The virgin who birthed kings.
I hold a small hand
spread butter and jam
stuff the freezer full of meat.
I've seen ovaries eaten—
breast sliced open.
I'm the one who bleeds.
There are mornings I cry
others I sing—

I'm the rye rising in the kitchen
drinking the sunlight and the yeast.

I thought I was ready to be a mother
Thought I understood the weight of the uterus
Its boundless waters

The Rain Fell, the Floods Came

> *my earthly / inheritance: your arms, your sigh, your heavy song*
> — Lee Herrick

I lost the lyric when I left my mother, entered
the fluorescent room.
I lost it with the first prick of the needle,

when the sun imploded
and became a hole I was pulled from.

I lost it in church when I sang to a room full of strangers,
head submerged in communal waters.

I lost the lyric when I opened my legs for a man
I will not name, for the earth
we ravage, my God,

his holy thumb pressing us into the dirt.
I lost it for a child yanked from in-between, a boy

who calls me mother—
asks I turn the world red as the uterus,

as the sky we come from, as the rock
I was told to stand on.
But I built my house on the sand, never listened

when they said the floods would come.
And he came and he came and he came
and a belly became a home became heavy with song.

The First Time

my son walked, he ran into the ocean.
I think he was trying to go home,
or at least someplace closer.

Whale Song

Did I tell you I found a whale fetus wrapped in seaweed?
Did I tell you the sockets were empty?
It was on a Monday.
The storm split a redwood in two and blocked
the road to Planned Parenthood.
Can you hear the orca sing?
The cries of the dying. She carried her dead calf
for seventeen days before releasing it.
Did I tell you my son's father poured water over my head
and left me in the forest?
Did I tell you he's an addict?
Did you know I unraveled the unborn whale,
stuffed it in my pocket?
Did you know the salmon are disappearing,
the whales are hungry, and the mother pushed
the calf a thousand miles with her head?

That Star, Right There

A mother punches a wall
until her knuckles bleed,

sticks her face
into a pillow and screams.
She looks at her son

and thinks love is so lonely,
at any moment he could be gone.

A mother prays death
will take her,
then begs forgiveness.

She couldn't leave her boy here,
alone.

Once a year
his father sends an email,
pours guilt like gasoline down her throat.

Why November?
She'll never know.

Maybe it's that winter is fated,
or is it the milk-white chill in the air?
But when a child asks, where's my dad?

Sometimes a mother points up
to the night. Sometimes a mother lies.

That You'd Disappear

I was thinking you'd never know your son
has your lisp when the radio announced bombs
dropped on a mosque.
The lost tang of your American Spirits
drifting through the vents.
God, you tasted good. What made me
come back that last time?
You threw my phone in poison oak—
and I walked Empire Grade with the night.
My hands never felt so small. Today, I lied.
Told him—there are snakes in that hole.
He didn't want to hear it but stayed away.
I wish I knew what was true. Our son doesn't
know he has a dad. Only I exist
and the memories we hold in a box
under the bed. How sad that we sleep off the past,
sadder still that we can't protect
those in prayer. Remember the last time?
He was only three months old. You returned
from Chumash Casino reeking of IPA
and organic cigarettes. I begged God,
one more wish.

How It Scattered Across the Lawn Like a Hand Tossing Seed

Someday, I'll tell my son why
we live with my parents.
Why Mommy works all the time.

I'll tell him he has a dad who lives in the forest
with a horse, Cadillac.
That the night we met, I rode bareback

through Big Basin, in the moonlight,
knew it was a part of a bigger plan.
Someday, I'll explain homelessness.

But he's a child
and he wants to build a nest.
So, I search "bird nest craft" and we scavenge

the yard for materials: twigs, loose hair and grasses,
try to follow the directions
and weave it all together.

I ask, what is the equivalent of a human nest?
He says a bed.
I think of all the nights

his feet have kicked me to the edge.
How my bed feels empty,
though my boy's next to me.

I didn't braid the twine tight enough
to the branch, and he screamed
as the wind unraveled it from the tree.

The Meadowlark

I feel guilty picking lavender,
and stepping on stones.
I see a ladybug land in my son's hair
and let it rest awhile.
A long-legged spider weaves a home into the corner.
A reoccurring dream
of a recluse in my bed, I try to kill it with a shoe
but it gets me first.
I'm the one the mosquitoes want to drink,
the sucker for love, the meat.
I see a cloud and think I could live here,
the sun is peeking through the pine
the vine is climbing the trunk.
We all need a host to carry us.

Sometimes I cry to the lark.
Sometimes I beg for its wings.

Water Song

Son,

The door you tore through
to get here is still bleeding.

I tried to warn you with each contraction,
my legs spread open. A mirror

at the edge of the bed.
Before I could look, I touched

your head with a finger,
didn't want to see my vagina that way,

didn't want to push
your face to the floor.

I almost held too tight, almost
squeezed you back

to death, to a song in water.
You said you remembered ripples.

Think of the body's brilliance,
how it found a way to you. How my hips

grew, how the tremors shook you out. Son,
I'm so sorry, I'm afraid,
I didn't want to bring you here. Afraid
of milk, of blood.

Veil of the Flower

Son,

I found your father face down
in chrysanthemum.

Can't stop seeing his bald head

the quarter moon
the blue sky.

Can't stop the odor

trapped gophers
fried hair.

This is love, I tell myself

a dead father
finally dead. Forgive me, I didn't cry,

didn't bury him in a casket.
I placed a sheet over the rot

and watered with gasoline.
Lit the outline

of a sunflower, offered it
like a lamb.

Cypress Cemetery

Black birds graze
in rows between headstones.
Yellowing grass sways
with westerly winds.
From a broken pine,
starling sing, and I
walk with the dead underneath—
as vultures winnow
in circles over me.
As if I'm the only
one here—slowly dying.

Tell me what it means—
The impossible thirst

About the Author

Kathryn de Lancellotti is a Pushcart Prize nominee and a former recipient of the Cowell Press Poetry Prize and the George Hitchcock Memorial Poetry Prize. Her poems and other works have appeared in *Chicago Quarterly Press Review, Catamaran Literary Reader, The American Journal of Poetry, Quarterly West, Cultural Weekly, Rust + Moth*, and others. Kathryn resides in Harmony, California, with her family.

Acknowledgements

The author would like to thank the editors of the following publications in which some of the poems first appeared, sometimes with a different title:

Bending Genres: "Whale Song"
Cultural Weekly: "Farewell to Jezebel: Eaten by Dogs"
Cultural Weekly: "Not to the Father Will I Give Myself," nominated for a Pushcart
Cultural Weekly: "These Walls"
Dodging the Rain: "The Rain Fell, The Floods Came"
Lady/Liberty/Lit: "Notre Dame Was on Fire, But Found Structurally Sound"
Lady/Liberty/Lit: "Things We Do"
Rabbid Oak: "Remember Me"
Rabbid Oak: "That You'd Disappear"
Rise Up Review: "A Daughter's Grief"
Rust + Moth: "Figure Study"
Softblow: "The Boot"
Softblow: "Clay and Pyre"
Softblow: "Homage to my Period"
Softblow: "The Astronaut and the Suit"
The Shore Poetry: "Meadowlark"
Typishly: "Veil of the Flower"

I would like to thank the following poets:

Gary Young, Luke Johnson, Laura Wetherington, Lee Herrick, Alexis Rhone Fancher, Eric Morago, Patricia Smith, Laura McCullough, Brian Turner, Gayle Brandeis, June Sylvester Saraceno, Shaun Griffin, Gerri Lucas, Katy Day, and Matthew Fleming.

Much love and gratitude to David Shannon for his well-honed editorial and aesthetic eye, for loving my son, and for the beautiful life we share.

Thanks also to my siblings: Stacey Kerstetter, Elizabeth Jones and David de Lancellotti for our bond and unconditional love. And to Liana Moynier, Lindsey Bolten, and Shelley Savoy for their sisterhood and lifelong friendship.

A very special thanks goes to my parents, Denise and Bobby de Lancellotti for helping raise my beautiful boy, Jayden—with all my love. And to Jayden, for the lessons he has taught me, for his unconditional love, and for his light.

Patrons

Moon Tide Press would like to thank the following people for their support in helping publish the finest poetry from the Southern California region. To sign up as a patron, visit www.moontidepress.com or send an email to publisher@moontidepress.com.

Anonymous
Robin Axworthy
Conner Brenner
Bill Cushing
Susan Davis
Peggy Dobreer
Dennis Gowans
Alexis Rhone Fancher
Hanalena Fennel
Half Off Books & Brad T. Cox
Jim & Vicky Hoggatt
Michael Kramer
Ron Koertge & Bianca Richards
Ray & Christi Lacoste
Zachary & Tammy Locklin
Lincoln McElwee
David McIntire
José Enrique Medina
Michael Miller & Rachanee Srisavasdi
Michelle & Robert Miller
Ronny & Richard Morago
Terri Niccum
Andrew November
Jennifer Smith
Andrew Turner
Rex Wilder
Mariano Zaro

Also Available from Moon Tide Press

Lullabies for End Times, Jennifer Bradpiece (2020)
Crabgrass World, Robin Axworthy (2020)
Contortionist Tongue, Dania Ayah Alkhouli (2020)
The only thing that makes sense is to grow, Scott Ferry (2020)
Dead Letter Box, Terri Niccum (2019)
Tea and Subtitles: Selected Poems 1999-2019, Michael Miller (2019)
At the Table of the Unknown, Alexandra Umlas (2019)
The Book of Rabbits, Vince Trimboli (2019)
Everything I Write Is a Love Song to the World, David McIntire (2019)
Letters to the Leader, HanaLena Fennel (2019)
Darwin's Garden, Lee Rossi (2019)
Dark Ink: A Poetry Anthology Inspired by Horror (2018)
Drop and Dazzle, Peggy Dobreer (2018)
Junkie Wife, Alexis Rhone Fancher (2018)
The Moon, My Lover, My Mother, & the Dog, Daniel McGinn (2018)
Lullaby of Teeth: An Anthology of Southern California Poetry (2017)
Angels in Seven, Michael Miller (2016)
A Likely Story, Robbi Nester (2014)
Embers on the Stairs, Ruth Bavetta (2014)
The Green of Sunset, John Brantingham (2013)
The Savagery of Bone, Timothy Matthew Perez (2013)
The Silence of Doorways, Sharon Venezio (2013)
Cosmos: An Anthology of Southern California Poetry (2012)
Straws and Shadows, Irena Praitis (2012)
In the Lake of Your Bones, Peggy Dobreer (2012)
I Was Building Up to Something, Susan Davis (2011)
Hopeless Cases, Michael Kramer (2011)
One World, Gail Newman (2011)
What We Ache For, Eric Morago (2010)
Now and Then, Lee Mallory (2009)
Pop Art: An Anthology of Southern California Poetry (2009)
In the Heaven of Never Before, Carine Topal (2008)
A Wild Region, Kate Buckley (2008)
Carving in Bone: An Anthology of Orange County Poetry (2007)
Kindness from a Dark God, Ben Trigg (2007)
A Thin Strand of Lights, Ricki Mandeville (2006)
Sleepyhead Assassins, Mindy Nettifee (2006)
Tide Pools: An Anthology of Orange County Poetry (2006)
Lost American Nights: Lyrics & Poems, Michael Ubaldini (2006)

www.ingramcontent.com/pod-product-compliance
Lightning Source LLC
Chambersburg PA
CBHW031219090426
42736CB00009B/979